THEORY WORK
FOR
INTERMEDIATE AND ADVANCED
TYPEWRITING EXAMINATIONS

Mary T. Robinson

A.F.T.Com., F.S.C.T.

Author of
*Exercises for Intermediate and Advanced
Typewriting Examinations*
Exercises for Elementary Typewriting Examinations
Typewriting by Easy Stages

CASSELL · LONDON

CASSELL & COMPANY LTD
35 Red Lion Square · London WC1R 4SJ

and at

SYDNEY · AUCKLAND
TORONTO · JOHANNESBURG

———

First edition April 1960
Second edition February 1961
Third edition July 1962
Fourth edition March 1963
Fifth (revised) edition March 1964
Sixth edition May 1965
Seventh (revised) edition 1969
Eighth (revised) edition 1972

I.S.B.N. 0 304 29057 2

PRINTED IN GREAT BRITAIN BY
THE CAMELOT PRESS LTD, LONDON AND SOUTHAMPTON
172

CONTENTS

iii

CHAPTER VI

CHAPTER VII

CHAPTER VIII

CHAPTER IX

CHAPTER X

CHAPTER XI

CHAPTER XII

PREFACE

This book is not intended for beginners or elementary students. It is designed for students intending to sit Intermediate and Advanced Examinations. It does not give examples, but the aim has been to put into as short a form as possible all the information that is required for these examinations, bringing out all the finer points of typewriting and giving short concise hints to students. Elementary information has been omitted as it is presumed students already possess this knowledge. Of the mechanism of the typewriter only the main parts have been covered. Nor does the book give a complete list of Commercial Abbreviations or any Legal Abbreviations. These can be found in various typewriting books usually provided in a class.

The book has intentionally been kept small so that it can be carried around easily and also studied at home, leaving class time to be devoted to practical work.

Since this book was originally published there has been a change in the style of exercises being set at examinations and sizes of paper used, although the basic theory remains the same. These alterations were incorporated in the seventh edition.

This edition includes more information with regard to modern layout.

ADVICE ON PREPARATION AND
EXAMINATION HINTS

Before entering for an examination make a complete study of previous examination papers. Work through as many papers as you can. Concentrate on each part until it has been thoroughly mastered, then proceed to work through the complete paper in the time allowed. The time element is an important factor and if you know you are capable of completing the paper within the time limit this will go a long way towards defeating "examination nerves". As well as working through previous papers obtain a good typewriting book and practise all types of exercises so that if a different type is introduced you are not at a loss as to how to handle it. Too many candidates enter for examinations with only a sketchy knowledge of their subject, or over-confident in their own ability. A certificate issued by a recognized Society indicates a typist's ability to do work at a certain standard and this is never gained without hard work, classes conscientiously attended, and a genuine interest in the subject.

The following points should be carefully noted, but more detailed information is to be found under the respective chapters.

Examination Bodies today differ greatly with regard to copying and accuracy tests. Some examinations still give the ten minutes' copying and accuracy tests. The R.S.A. give a small copying test and students "are advised to spend no longer than five minutes on this test". There is no accuracy test but a candidate is expected to be able to type at 25, 35 or 50 w.p.m. before entering for the appropriate examination. Again some examinations give only a ten minutes' accuracy test. There are different rules according to the examination as to how these tests should be typed and students are advised to read the instructions carefully with regard to line-spacing, margins and length of line required as the variations are too many to state here.

If an accuracy test is included, aim for absolute accuracy. Do not start off in a rush or be influenced by the speed of others around you. This test is a combination of speed and accuracy, but accuracy is the most important. The slower, but more accurate, typist will often gain more marks here. Type on the top half of the ribbon because the ribbon does not need to rise so high for each stroke, thereby increasing speed. Everything that is not perfect is marked as an error, e.g. letters too lightly typed, uneven right and left-hand margins, wrongly divided words at line ends, two spaces between words, typing too far down the paper, letters, words or lines inserted or omitted, wrong spacing after punctuation marks, wrong paragraph indenting, letters overlapping, shift keys not depressed sufficiently causing letters to be out of alignment, dash incorrectly rendered, wrong line spacing, and overtyping. If the test runs on to a second page place a pencil mark on the "copy" to indicate the last word typed so that when the second page is commenced no time is lost looking for the place. Never use a catchword. The test is required to be typed *once* only, in 10 minutes, and no marks are gained for beginning it a second time. An eraser must *not* be used in this test.

If a business letter occurs, read the instructions to see whether or not a carbon copy is required. Make sure the date is not omitted. If the letter is intended to occupy one page do not commence too far down the paper, especially in advanced examinations. If an enclosure is mentioned do not omit the word "Enc.". Sometimes this is not indicated on the test paper, but a small pencil mark placed in the margin opposite the line wherein the enclosure is mentioned will help to remind you. If no instructions are given any method of display will be accepted. Leave only two lines between the last line and the complimentary close. Erase all mistakes, but do it neatly. Read through before passing on to the next test. See under "Letters" for correct setting out.

A manuscript test is invariably included and it is absolutely essential to read the instructions carefully before commencing to type. Again there is no need to rush. Read the exercise, or at least a part of it, to become familiar with the handwriting and subject matter. Be careful in tracing the lines from "ballooned" portions so that the encircled words are typed in the correct place. It is better to get these and transposed portions in their correct place, even if this means the exercise is not finished, than to finish the whole exercise badly. More marks are often gained if exercises are incomplete but correctly typed than if the whole matter is finished but badly typed. Be careful with regard to indentation, and all reference marks must be produced by means of typewritten combination characters. If in doubt as to the setting out of any manuscript work use the test paper as a guide. Do not type on both sides of the paper. Never overtype, never have untidy erasures or type words in the abbreviated form, and never use a catchword. See under "Displayed and Manuscript Work" (p. 37) for further particulars.

For a tabular statement the following should be noted. Work out calculations slowly, be accurate with the centring of headings, and have the same margins at each side and the same amount of blank space at top and bottom. In R.S.A. Examinations ruling may be done entirely in ink, or by use of the underscore, or by a mixture of both methods. The work is intended to occupy one page only. Again all reference marks must be produced by means of typewritten combination characters. No abbreviated forms are allowed except perhaps in a column heading, and if any item in the particulars' column extends to a second line this line is indented two spaces. Remember to insert leader dots if required. See under "Tabular Work" for fuller instructions.

If there are questions to be answered draft the answers first. Do not ramble, but on the other hand do not omit the point of the question—give short clear answers.

Use a separate sheet of paper for each test. Place your name or examination number on each sheet and do not type first all the easiest parts which often carry the least marks. And finally, if you are half-way or more through an exercise and make a very bad mistake—such as leaving out a line—do not immediately commence that exercise again thinking you can rush through it quickly. You will only become flustered. Stop it at once and carry on with the remainder of the paper. If time permits it can be retyped at the end.

Examination Materials: Take to the examination a ruler, pen, pencil, soft eraser and typewriter eraser, blotting paper, ink, paper clips or pins, carbon paper and a few sheets of paper for practice. Paper for the actual examination is provided. You can supply your own typewriter for some examinations.

Practice: Be in the examination room at least a quarter of an hour before the examination commences in order to familiarize yourself with the machine or adjust your chair.

Defects: If your typewriter develops a fault report this immediately to the Supervisor, who will either arrange for another typewriter to be supplied or make a note on your paper.

Spoilt Sheets: If a sheet has been spoilt draw an oblique line through the work and commence on a new sheet. Make sure you do not type on the back of a cancelled sheet and hand in any spoilt sheets.

Worked Papers: If you finish before the time is up resist the temptation to hand in your work. Spend up to the last minute reading through all worked papers so that no mistakes are left uncorrected. Also make sure that all work is handed in.

CHAPTER I

1. HOW AN EXPERT OPERATOR IS PRODUCED

Use the touch method because it produces the highest speed in the shortest time. Have continual practice under a competent teacher on a good machine. Type long unfamiliar words from beginning to end without hesitation. Keep the carriage moving steadily all the time, and not by fits and starts. Jot down in a notebook all words which give particular trouble, and type them until thoroughly mastered. Never allow anxiety for high speed to interfere with neat and accurate work. Aim for accuracy and try to type each page more correctly than the last. Acquire confidence and speed will come.

2. TIME-SAVING HINTS

Sit correctly and comfortably.

Use correct fingering and the touch system.

Keep the hands close to the keys, with the fingers curved and the little fingers over the Guide Keys.

Let the wrists and hands be as still as possible and do not move the arms in making the strokes.

Remove paper with the right hand, and insert a fresh sheet with the left quickly and straight.

Return the carriage smartly with one hand—it is not necessary to accompany the carriage all the way.

Bring hands back quickly to the keyboard.

Use correct shift keys and never cross hands.

Type on the *top* half of the ribbon for speed tests.

Keep your eyes continually on the copy, never look at the keyboard.

Listen for the warning bell.

Indicate on paper with a pencil mark where the last line of typing is to finish—about one inch from the bottom.

At the conclusion of a page mark with a pencil on the printed copy the last word typed.

3. GOOD TYPING

Uniform impressions and spacing, well-centred headlines, no over-types, mis-spellings, wrongly divided words at line-ends, omissions, insertions or faulty timing of shift keys, and no dirty erasures. The matter should be accurate and displayed tastefully.

4. DEVELOPMENT OF SPEED

Good physical and mental condition.

Practice on the right lines.

Access to a good typewriter.

Machine kept oiled and free from faults.

Confidence and power of concentration.

Touch method and correct degree of touch—neither too heavy nor too light—

Heavy touch retards.

Light does not give necessary rebound.

Even timing of depressions.

Eyes must never leave the matter which is being copied.

Typing alphabetical sentences—each sentence containing the letters of the entire alphabet.

Typing long and difficult words.

Typing faulty stretch exercises.

Double letter exercises.

Drilling on words presenting difficulty.

Drilling on special characters, e.g. *inverted commas, brackets, hyphen,* etc.

Repetition of familiar passages.

Typing passages for 5, 10 and 15 minutes.

CHAPTER II

1. MAIN PARTS OF TYPEWRITER

1. KEYBOARD—Consists of four rows of keys—10 or 11 in a row—space bar in front.
2. TYPE BASKET—Contains type-bars to which are fixed metal types so that the desired characters are, one after another, in any order typed on the paper.
3. INKING DEVICE—Inking is accomplished by a ribbon against which the types strike.
4. CARRIAGE—This contains the cylinder which holds the paper in the correct position for writing and by its movements provides for the spacing of the letters and lines. After a key is struck the carriage travels from right to left the width of a letter.
5. MAINSPRING AND ESCAPEMENT—The motive power which moves the carriage is imparted by an adjustable coiled spring and the spacing of the letters is governed by the escapement.
6. DRAWBAND—The tape or band which connects the carriage with the carriage tension spring.
7. CARRIAGE RELEASE LEVERS—These are levers for quickly moving the carriage from one position to another independently of the escapement.
8. CYLINDER—Platen or large roller in the centre of the carriage against which the types strike.
9. PLATEN—Alternative name for cylinder.

10. CYLINDER KNOBS—The hand wheels at either end of the cylinder with which to revolve the cylinder by hand.
11. CARRIAGE RETURN AND LINE SPACE LEVER—The lever, usually on the left of the carriage, for returning the carriage and turning paper to next line of writing in one operation.
12. LINE SPACE REGULATOR—A device for regulating the line spacing for single, double and treble spacing.
13. PAPER RELEASE LEVER—For releasing the pressure on the feed rolls for adjustment or removal of paper from machine.
14. FEED ROLLS—Small rollers, beneath the cylinder, which hold the paper close to the cylinder.
15. VARIABLE LINE SPACER—A knob on the end of the cylinder which releases the line space rachet from the cylinder and allows any width of line spacing to be used. For typing on ruled lines.
16. PLATEN RELEASE LEVER—Has same effect as Variable Line Spacer but when re-engaged the platen will automatically return to *exact* point of original writing. Used for raising letters.
17. MARGIN REGULATORS—The stops used for setting right and left-hand margins.
18. MARGIN RELEASE—A key which temporarily releases both margins or on some machines the left-hand margin only to allow work to be typed in margin or margins.
19. LINE LOCK RELEASE—Another name for Margin Release, but acts at the *end* of lines only to allow typing to be continued into right-hand margin.
20. PAPER TABLE—The support behind the platen on which the paper rests.
21. KEY RELEASE LEVER—For releasing type bars when two or more become "jammed" due to a mis-stroke. Only on some makes of machine.
22. PRINTING POINT or COMMON CENTRE—The place where all the types converge and strike the platen.

There are two types of electric typewriter: the standard electric typewriter, which does not differ from the manual typewriter except in the method of operation—key depression, carriage return and line spacing are all electrically controlled—and the IBM 72, which has no typebars. The 88 characters are mounted on a small typing head, the size of a golf ball. This ball, and not the carriage, moves along when the keys are depressed. When a key is struck, the head tilts and rotates to bring the proper character into position for typing. Only six hundredths of a second elapse from striking a key to printing a character. The typing head can be changed quite easily for another of a different type style.

2. SIZES OF TYPE

Inch basis

Pica Type	.. ..	10 letters to the inch across and 6 lines to the inch down. Used for business purposes.
Elite Type	.. ..	12 letters to the inch across and 6 lines to the inch down. Used for business and private work.
Petit Roman Type	..	16 letters to the inch across and 8 lines to the inch down. Used to imitate printed matter.
Pin Point Type	..	10 letters to the inch across. Used for cheques. Each character perforates the paper to prevent subsequent alteration of words and figures.

Metric basis

Pica Type	.. ..	3.902 letters to 1 centimetre
Elite Type	.. ..	4.8 letters to 1 centimetre
Petit Roman Type	..	6 letters to 1 centimetre
Line spacing	.. ..	4.2 mm equals one line space
		25 mm equals six lines

With the present typewriters the above figures require to be rounded off.

3. KINDS OF RIBBONS

Record or Non-copying: Ribbons inked with a fast dye which makes them absolutely permanent. They are made in a wide variety of colours and are best for ordinary work as corrections are easier and neater. A *black* record is always used for legal documents.

Bi-chrome (Two coloured): These are a combination of two colours—usually black and red. When red is one of the colours it is used for credit notes, to emphasize headings or special words, and for cues and stage directions in plays.

Copying: Usually purple and used for all work which has to be press copied.

Litho: This is a ribbon which contains "grease" and is used when typing paper plates for the Offset Litho duplicating process.

Carbon: The ribbon in this case is a roll of carbon paper, usually slightly narrower than the normal width of a ribbon and approximately 650 feet (198 metres) long. It produces good work but it can only be used once.

4. SIZES OF TYPEWRITING PAPER

			Width	Length	Width	Length
Octavo	..	..	..	5″ × 8″		
Quarto	..	..	..	8″ × 10″		
Foolscap	..	..	..	8″ × 13″		
Draft	..	..	..	10″ × 16″		
Brief	..	..	..	13″ × 16″		
A5	..	..	..	$5\frac{7}{8}″$ × $8\frac{1}{4}″$ (approx.)	148 mm × 210 mm	
A4	..	..	..	$8\frac{1}{4}″$ × $11\frac{3}{4}″$ (approx.)	210 mm × 297 mm	

A ream has 500 sheets: a quire 25 sheets.

Characters and lines in A5 and A4 paper (approx.)

Type				Across	Down	A5		A4	
						(used vertically)			
				Letters to the inch	Lines to the inch	Letters Across	Lines Down	Letters Across	Lines Down
Pica	..	..	..	10	6	59	50	82	70
Elite	..	..	..	12	6	71	50	99	70
						(used horizontally)			
Pica	..	..	..			82	35		
Elite	..	..	..			99	35		

5. MAIN USES OF VARIOUS SIZES OF PAPER

Octavo —Short business letters, private letters, short invoices, monthly statements, memos and actors' parts of plays.

Quarto —Business letters, invoices, plays and all literary work.

Foolscap —Reports, specifications, agendas, minutes and legal drafts.

Draft —Legal documents and legal accounts.

Brief —Barristers' briefs, abstracts of title, financial statements, balance sheets and large business accounts.

A5 —Short business letters, invoices, statements, order forms, memos, credit and debit notes and actors' parts of plays.

A4 —Business letters, reports, specifications, agendas, minutes, plays, literary work and tabulated statements.

CHAPTER III

1. Typescript Corrections
2. Combination Characters

3. Commercial Signs
4. Typing Metric

1. TYPESCRIPT CORRECTIONS

caps.   Marks used in the →   *centre*
          Correction of Manuscript and Typescript, etc. →

The highroad along which we had travelled from Falmouth
runs inland from the sea coast It follows the bend of the coast
u.c. as this turns in to form the wide mouth of the helford River.
From the road the land slopes down to the water in a number of
lovely combes, heavily wooded, and land owners thereabouts
have often seen the beauty of these little valleys as housing sites.
Tresco Vean was the loveliest of these houses. It was built of
l.c. grey crumbly Cornish Stone, reinforced in doorways and at all
angles with granite.
It stood upon a platform at the head of the valley, and from here
the land ran down steeply to the water. On either side were
beechwoods; within them green thickets of rhododendron and
camelia, hydrangea and fuchsia; and within these again was the
long grassy walk to the water.
Par. Often enough during storms at sea my thoughts would turn back
to that delectable place and I would wonder at the arrangement
of mens affairs which permitted one to remain snugly there
propped in his security by the danger and desperate action of
N.P. others such as I. But when I had flung out of Tresco Vean that
stet night, it was not of such things that I was thinking.

The undernoted are the most common marks used in proof correcting given in the order in which they appear in the passage on the previous page.

Marks in
Margin   *Meaning*

Caps	Together with the double underscoring indicates that the words are to be in capitals.
→ Centre	Heading to be centred.
⊢⊣	Dash to be inserted at points indicated.
just	The word to be inserted as indicated.
⊙	Insert full stop.
trs.	Transpose the two letters marked.
u.c. (meaning upper case)	Capital for initial H.
⌒	Close up.
∂	Delete (take out) the word crossed through.
H	Hyphen to be inserted at place indicated.
l.c. (meaning lower case) ..	Small letter for s.
run on	No fresh paragraph.
trs.	Transpose the two words marked.
#	Space required at place indicated.
l/	Letter 'l' to be inserted.
s/	Letter 's' to be inserted.
Par.	New paragraph where indicated by square bracket.
'/	Apostrophe to be inserted where shown.
,/	Comma to be inserted where indicated.
N.P.	New paragraph where indicated by square bracket.
stet.	Together with dots under the word crossed out means that it is to remain as it was.

2. COMBINATION CHARACTERS

These are characters formed by the use of two existing characters. Either back space or hold down the space bar while typing both characters. It is sometimes necessary to use the platen release lever to allow the characters to be raised or lowered.

Dollar	By using the capital S and oblique sign			₷
Cent	,, ,, ,, capital or small c and oblique sign			₵ ¢
Section Mark	,, ,, ,, two large or small s's one typed slightly above the other			§ §
Equation	,, ,, ,, two hyphens			=
Caret	,, ,, ,, oblique sign and underscore			⟋

Division	By using the colon and hyphen	÷
Asterisk	,, ,, ,, small x and hyphen	✳
Dagger	,, ,, ,, capital I and hyphen	⸸
Double Dagger	,, ,, ,, capital I and two hyphens or capital I and equation sign	⹋
Exclamation Mark	,, ,, ,, apostrophe and full stop	!
Per cent	,, ,, ,, small o, oblique sign, o	o/o
Mille	,, ,, ,, small o, oblique sign, oo	o/oo
Degree	,, ,, ,, small o raised	40°
Semi-colon	,, ,, ,, colon and comma	;
Cedilla	,, ,, ,, comma under the small c	ç
Square Brackets	,, ,, ,, oblique sign and underscore	⌐ ¬
Diaeresis	,, ,, ,, quotation sign	ü

The plus sign cannot be obtained satisfactorily unless already provided on the keyboard and should be made with pen and ink.

When typing stencils the letter 't' can be used for the plus sign by slightly lowering and obliterating the bottom curve.

The following are not combination characters
but are given for information.

Feet	By using the apostrophe	11'
Inches	,, ,, ,, quotation sign	4″
Minutes	,, ,, ,, apostrophe	12'
Seconds	,, ,, ,, quotation sign	40″
Dash	,, ,, ,, hyphen with a space before and after	—
Decimal Point	,, ,, ,, full stop either raised or on the same line	1.5
Minus	,, ,, ,, hyphen	2 – 1
Multiplication	,, ,, ,, small x	2 × 6
Brace	,, ,, ,, brackets	(or)
		( )
		( )

3. COMMERCIAL SIGNS

& (ampersand) represents the sign for "and" and is used only

(i) in the names of firms, e.g. *Messrs Jones & Brown*

The name of a firm should not be divided at the end of a line. If it is a short title try to get it all in or take it all to the next line.

(ii) in the numbers of an address, e.g. 4 & 5 *High Street*

(iii) in certain abbreviations, e.g. E. & O.E., C. & F.

The ampersand must *never* be used for the word "and" in the body of the text.

@ (at) stands for "at", "at the price of", and "for" and is used only in the typing of invoices, estimates, etc., but never in correspondence.

£ (Libra) is the pound sign and it should never be followed by a period as it is not an abbreviation but a symbol.

— (underscore) is used to underline subject headings, titles and sub-titles in display work, titles of books, magazines, newspapers, plays, ships, etc.; to emphasize words or phrases which otherwise would be written in italics; for foreign words, for ruled lines at the foot of a column of figures as invoices; to indicate thousands in Roman Numerals ($\overline{V}$ = 5,000) and for square brackets in conjunction with the oblique sign /. If the underscore looks broken, lock the shift key and while striking the underscore move the ribbon along by turning the ribbon spool.

% (per cent) must be used only with a figure—5%—and no space should be left between the figure and sign. Where space permits it is better to use the words "per cent" with no period following.

/ oblique is used to represent the word "*to*" in numbers, e.g. 60/66; in sloping fractions, as 7/8*ths*; as a contraction for "*the*" in manuscript; and as an alternative to the caret to show an omission.

4. TYPING METRIC

Metre	..	..	..	.. By using small m	.. 1 m
Centimetre	..	..	..	,, ,, a small c and m	.. 14 cm
Millimetre	..	..	..	,, ,, two small m's	.. 26 mm
Kilometre	..	..	..	,, ,, a small k and m	.. 13 km
Gramme	..	..	..	,, ,, a small g	.. 85 g
Kilogramme	..	..	..	,, ,, a small k and g	.. 25 kg
Litre	..	..	..	.. Always type the word in full ..	1 litre
Tonne	..	..	..	,, ,, ,, ,, ,, ,, ..	1 tonne

Note: There is always one space left after a figure and no full stop between or after the letter or letters.

CHAPTER IV

1. ROMAN NUMERALS

1 =	I	10 =	X
2 =	II	50 =	L
3 =	III	100 =	C
4 =	IV	500 =	D
5 =	V	1,000 =	M

A stroke above multiplies a number by 1,000, e.g. 6,000 = $\overline{\text{VI}}$ 1,000,000 = $\overline{\text{M}}$. If difficulty is experienced in memorizing the higher symbols try this memory aid. Remember that CD and LM occur together in the alphabet. M is the highest letter used and 1,000 the highest figure employed. Split the L and M and insert the CD between and place the arabic figures opposite, i.e.

$$
\begin{array}{ll}
\underline{L =} & 50 \\
\underline{C =} & 100 \\
\underline{D =} & 500 \\
M = & 1,000
\end{array}
$$

When working out Roman Numerals take each figure by itself:

25 = 20 + 5 = XX + V = XXV
82 = 50 + 30 + 2 = L + XXX + II = LXXXII
536 = 500 + 30 + 6 = D + XXX + VI = DXXXVI
1958 = 1,000 + 900 + 50 + 8 = M + CM + L + VIII = MCMLVIII

Please note that 4, 9, 40, 90, 400 and 900 are the only numbers where a higher number is taken and the corresponding difference placed in front as a subtraction. Only one symbol can be placed in front of any other symbol.

$$4 = 5 - 1 = IV$$
$$9 = 10 - 1 = IX$$
$$40 = 50 - 10 = XL$$
$$90 = 100 - 10 = XC$$
$$400 = 500 - 100 = CD$$
$$900 = 1,000 - 100 = CM$$

When compiling any other number add on the symbols.

Large Roman Numerals are used:

1. In numbering chapters and headings.
2. In enumerating paragraphs.
3. For the year.
4. For monarchs, and class and form numbers.
5. For the books of the Bible.

Small Roman Numerals are used for paginating prefaces and sub-paragraphs. Roman Numerals are not followed by a full stop unless numbering paragraphs.

2. FIGURES AND WORDS

Figures are used:

1. For numbers including and over 10 in general work.
2. For numbers including and over 100 in literary work.
3. For dates, distances, weights, measurements, votes, house numbers and degrees of heat.
4. With the " % " sign, e.g. 4%
5. When using a.m. and p.m., e.g. 10 *a.m.*, 4 *p.m.*
6. For numbers in postcodes, e.g. *EH4 2JZ*
7. For numbering policies or certificates.
8. After the abbreviation *No.* for number.
9. For scores in games and matches.

Words are used:

1. For numbers one to nine inclusive in general work.
2. For numbers under 100 in literary work.
3. When a sentence begins with a number, e.g. *Five hundred men were present.*
4. For time when using the word "o'clock", e.g. *five o'clock.*

5. For cheques, receipts, estimates and legal documents where accuracy is important.

6. When expressing a number in an indefinite manner, e.g. *There were about eight hundred books in the library.*

7. When referring to population or quantity, e.g.
   The largest town has over six million inhabitants.
   Only fifty per cent of the forms were returned.

3. PERIOD, INVERTED COMMAS (DOUBLE QUOTATION MARKS) AND APOSTROPHE (SINGLE QUOTATION MARK)

The period, or full stop, is used:

1. At the end of a sentence.

2. For abbreviated forms, thus—*i.e., e.g., Co., Vol., G.P.O.,* but is never used after the following: *re, per, via,* as these are not abbreviations but Latin forms. There is also no period after Ordinal Numbers (1*st*, 2*nd*, etc.).

3. After Christian initials and letters representing degrees:
   J. J. Brown, Esq., M.A.

4. As leader dots in tabular work in order to guide the eye from column to column.

5. For the decimal point which does not necessarily require to be raised.

6. After figures or letters enumerating paragraphs. Always leave two spaces before commencing a paragraph.

7. To indicate the omission of some words. Three spaced points are sufficient.

8. To separate hours and minutes, e.g. 4.30 *p.m.*

9. To separate dollars and cents, e.g. $30.30

10. To separate pounds and pence, e.g. £40.50

Although the above uses of the full stop are still in common practice, some examination papers are being set using "open punctuation". In this case the full stop would not be used after or between:

1. Familiar abbreviations—ie, eg, pm, GPO, UNO

2. Christian initials and degrees—J J Brown Esq MA

3. Figures or letters enumerating paragraphs. Leave three or four spaces before commencing paragraph, depending on size of type.

Inverted commas, or double quotation marks, are used for:

1. A direct quotation.

2. The ditto sign.

3. Inches.

4. Seconds in geographical measurement, e.g. 40° 4″ *N. Lat.*

5. Denoting extracts. When the extract or quotation consists of several paragraphs the quotation marks should be placed at the beginning of each paragraph but at the end of the last one only. In poetry they should be placed at the beginning of the first verse and at the end of the last.
6. The names of books, magazines, newspapers, plays, ships, etc.

Apostrophe, or single quotation mark, is used for:

1. The possessive case.
2. A quotation within a quotation.
3. An omission, e.g. *don't.*
4. Foot or feet.
5. Minutes in geographical measurements, e.g. 40° 4′.
6. Plurals of letters and figures, e.g.
   > *Dot your i's and cross your t's.*
   > *There are two 9's in the total.*

   Note: In a direct quotation the final quotation marks are placed *outside the* comma, period, question mark, etc. If a phrase or word only is being quoted the final quotation mark is placed *inside* the punctuation because it is the whole sentence and not just the quoted part that requires the punctuation, e.g. "What are you doing?" It is hard to "see ourselves as others see us". "Did you say 'come'?"

4. DIVISION OF WORDS AT LINE-ENDS

When dividing a word at the end of a line use the hyphen and the hyphen only. Never commence the following line with a colon and never divide words on more than two consecutive lines. The following rules should be memorized:

1. Divide between natural syllables. Pronounce the word and listen to the way it falls into syllables, e.g. *struc-ture, engross-ment, micro-scope, speci-men* Syllables usually commence with a consonant—except certain endings like *-ing, -able, -est* and *-ish*, e.g. *cheat-ing, prefer-able, earli-est, self-ish.* It is not permissible to take endings of two letters to the next line, e.g. *ed* and *ly* or to leave one or two letters at the end of a line, e.g. *re* and *a.*
2. Words of one syllable or their plurals are not divided, e.g. *there, pieces.*
3. In words commencing with a prefix divide after the prefix, e.g. *intro-duce, con-dition.*
4. In words ending with a suffix divide before the suffix, e.g. *harm-less, situa-tion.*
5. When double consonants occur in the middle of a word divide between them, e.g. *neces-sary, inter-rupted.*

6. When three consonants come together in the middle of a word divide before or after the consonants that must be pronounced together, e.g *crumbling, chil-dren, bank-ruptcy*.

7. When the final consonant of a root word is doubled for the addition of a suffix divide between the two consonants, e.g. *occur-ring, forget-ting*.

8. Compound words and words already containing a hyphen cannot be divided a second time but can be split where the hyphen occurs, e.g. *hasty-tempered, pre-eminent*.

9. The last word of a page should not be divided.

10. Any set of figures should not be divided, e.g. 14 m × 3 m

11. Do not separate title from name nor the initials of a name, e.g. *Mr* from *Brown* or *Mr W.* from *T. Smith*. Carry over name in full to next line.

12. Proper names are not divided, e.g. *Manchester, Brittany*.

A list of prefixes and suffixes can be found at the end of most dictionaries.

5. HALF-SPACE CORRECTING

It is possible to substitute a longer word for a shorter, such as "have" for "had". There are three different ways in which it can be done.

Method 1: Erase the incorrect word. Place the carriage where the first letter
had   had been written. Space once. Hold the back spacer all the way
have   down. Type the first letter. For each subsequent letter of the
          word, space twice, hold the back spacer and type the letter.

Method 2: Erase the incorrect word. Place the carriage where the first letter
          had been written, then release the paper and move it half a space
          along to the right, type the word and then move the paper back to
          its original position. This method takes longer.

Method 3: Erase the incorrect word. Place the carriage where the first letter
          had been written, hold down back spacer half way and type the
          required letter. For each subsequent letter hold down back spacer
          half way and type the letter.

In each case there is only half a space before and after the word instead of a full space.

To spread or balance a shorter word in the space used for a longer word, such as "had" for "have", the methods are similar.

Method 1: After erasing the word place the carriage where the first letter had
have   been written. Space twice and hold down the back spacer. Type
had   the first letter. For each subsequent letter space twice, hold down
          the back spacer and type the letter.

Method 2: The same as Method 2 above but move the paper half a space to the left.

Method 3: The same as Method 3 above but place the carriage where the second letter had been written.

In each case there is a space and a half before and after the word instead of only one space.

CHAPTER V

1. LITERARY DEFINITIONS

Draft: The first copy of a document typed in treble spacing, on one side of the paper only, to allow for corrections.

Fair Copy: This is the corrected draft retyped. It is typed in double spacing on one side of the paper and there should be no mistakes or abbreviations.

Foul Proof: Is a printer's term meaning a proof marked with many errors.

Short Page: This is the term used when the last page of a document has less than the full quantity of matter, e.g. chapters of books.

Dropped Heads: This means commencing further down the page than the normal line of typing, e.g. chapter headings.

Tail Piece: Is a decorative ending to an article, book chapter or section.

Break Line: This is the last line of a paragraph—if it is a short line—and the break is the division into a fresh paragraph.

Hanging Paragraph: The first line of the paragraph commences at the margin or a predetermined position and second and subsequent lines indented a few spaces.

Indented Paragraph: The first line indented and following lines brought back to the margin.

Block Paragraph: All lines, including the first, commence at margin or same degree of scale.

Side or Marginal Notes: Are notes placed in the margin.

Centre Notes: A space is often left between two columns of matter wherein centre notes are written.

Headlines: This is a printer's term covering the lines at the top of a page with running title, pagination, etc.

Running Headlines: When the headlines continue from page to page.

Head: The blank space left at the top of a page.

Head Word: This is the term used for the word forming a heading.

Title Page: The page of a book which contains name of book, name of author and name of publisher.

Half Title: This is the first page of a book coming before the title page and contains the name of the book only.

Hook-in: This is a term used mainly in the typing of poetry. If there are too many words in a line in comparison with the other lines the extra words are placed above or below their own line, e.g.

To the noise of the mourning of a mighty
(nation,

Fit: When a manuscript is divided among several typists it must be so divided that the last line of each portion comes to the bottom of a page in order that it may "fit", without a break, to the following sheet. If difficulty is experienced in making it "fit in" the line spacing of the last page may be altered. *Dove-tailing* is an alternative word for "fit".

2. LEGAL DEFINITIONS

Draft: The first copy of a legal document. Typed in treble spacing on one side of foolscap or A4 paper. Dates and sums of money may be typed in figures. The word "draft" should appear on the endorsement.

Clean Draft or Fair Copy: The corrected draft of a document retyped in double spacing still on one side of foolscap or A4 paper. Figures may again be used and the word "draft" should also appear on the endorsement.

Engrossment: This is the name given to a deed when it is finally typed for signature by a client. Typed in double spacing on both sides of double draft or brief paper and the last page left blank for endorsement when the document is folded. No abbreviations or erasures must occur and all names, dates and sums of money must be typed in full.

Counterpart: A duplicate of the engrossment.

Endorsement: This is typed on the last outside page of a legal document and should contain date, names of parties, brief description of contents and name of solicitor.

Copy: When a copy is made of a legal document the word "copy" should precede the name of the deed on the endorsement and the word "signed" should be placed before the signature to the document.

Affidavit: Is a written declaration on oath given before a magistrate or notary public.

Agreement: Is a contract between two people.

Brief: Is a written statement of a client's case in a law suit.

Statement of Claim: Is a document setting out fully the rights of the claimant.

Defendant: Is the party in any legal case sued at law.

Plaintiff: Is the party in any legal case who commences an action at law.

Disposition: Is a document making over property.

Lease: A document dealing with the letting of houses or lands for a specific time at a specified rent.

Will: A document setting out the express wishes of any person as to the administration and disposal of his possessions after his death.

Holograph Will: A Will written entirely in a person's own handwriting.

Locus Sigilli: Place of the seal.

Inter Alia: Among other things.

Testimonium Clause: Is the clause placed at the end of legal documents starting "IN WITNESS whereof" against which the parties sign their names. (English form of law.)

Attestation Clause: Is the clause following the Testimonium Clause commencing "SIGNED, SEALED AND DELIVERED" against which the witnesses sign their names. (English form of law.)

Testing Clause: Is the last clause in a Scottish Legal Document commencing "IN WITNESS whereof". In Scotland there is not a separate Testimonium Clause and Attestation Clause—the two being combined in one clause which includes the names of the parties signing, place and date of signing, and names, designations and addresses of witnesses.

3. 100 COMMON ABBREVIATIONS

A/C	account current	B/R	bills receivable
A/c	account	B/S	bill of sale
a/d	after date	B.S.	balance sheet
ad lib.	at pleasure	c/d	carried down
ad val.	according to value	cf.	compare
a.m.	before noon	c/f	carried forward
amt.	amount	c.f.i.	cost, freight and insurance
A/S	account sales		
b/d	brought down	ch.	chapter
B/E	bill of exchange	chq.	cheque
b/f	brought forward	c.i.f.	cost, insurance and freight
B/L	bill of lading		
B/P	bills payable	circa.	about

cm	centimetre	MS.	manuscript
c/o	care of	MSS.	manuscripts
C.O.D.	cash on delivery	N.B.	take note, mark well
con.	against	nem. con.	no one contradicting
cr.	credit, creditor	net	lowest
cum. div.	with dividend	No., Nos.	number, numbers
curt.	this month	8vo	octavo
dept.	department	para	paragraph
dis.	discount	per	by
divd.	dividend	per ann.	yearly
do.	the same	per cent	by the hundred
D/O	delivery order	per pro.	on behalf of
Dr.	doctor, debtor	p.m.	afternoon
E. & O.E.	errors and omissions excepted	p	pence
		p.	per, page
E.E.	errors excepted	pp.	pages
e.g.	for example	pro	for
etc.	and so on	pro and con.	for and against
et seq.	and the following	pro forma	as a matter of form
ex.	out of	pro tem.	for the time being
fcp.	foolscap	prox.	next month
f.o.b.	free on board	PS.	postscript
fol.	folio	PPS.	a second postscript
f.o.r.	free on rail	Qto 4to	quarto
ft.	foot, feet	q.v.	which see
fwd.	forward	re	with reference to
h.p.	horse-power	R.S.V.P.	please reply
ib.	in the same place	s.d.	indefinitely
id.	the same	seq.	the following
i.e.	that is	SS.	steamship
in.	inch, inches	st.	stet—let it stand
inst.	this month	s.v.	under the heading
IOU	I owe you	ult.	last month
i.q.	the same as	v.	versus (against)
L.S.	the place of the seal	via	by way of
Ltd	Limited	viz.	videlicet (namely)
Messrs	Gentlemen, Sirs	vol.	volume
MM.	Messieurs	x.d.	ex (without) dividend
mo., mos.	month, months		

CHAPTER VI

1. Commercial Letters
2. Official Letters
3. Envelope Addressing
4. Titles and Forms of Address

1. COMMERCIAL LETTERS

Traditional

The following are points which often give rise to difficulty:

Reference and date must be on the same line unless a special place is provided for the reference. If there are two references, line date up with the lower one. There should be no period after the reference.

Date must line up with right-hand margin. In the case of March, April, May, June and July it should commence $1\frac{1}{2}$ inches to the left of the right-hand margin, and for the other months 2 inches to the left. Never use figures, e.g. 22.1.72.

Christian initials may be typed with or without a space between, but no space is required between abbreviations after a name.

The sign "&" must never be used except in the name of a company and between numbers in an address. In all other cases type "and" in full.

Never abbreviate "Street" or "Road", etc.

If no indication is given as to whether an address has to be blocked or indented, the blocked method is quicker and more up-to-date. If there is a postcode always include it.

Subject headings must be centred over the width of the letter, not the width of the paper, with no full stop unless the heading finishes with an abbreviated word like "Co.".

Never underline punctuation marks.

Particulars "inset" must be inset equally from each margin making a compact square or oblong in the centre of the letter, and always typed in single spacing.

Always use the "hyphen" to divide words at the end of the line and never use a "colon" at the commencement of the following line. Do not hyphenate on more than two consecutive lines.

Figures from 1 to 9 appearing in the text should be typed in words unless they apply to measurements, weights or distances. From 10 upwards they are typed as figures.

Type all abbreviated words in full.

Never use a catchword in a commercial letter.

If an enclosure is mentioned type "Enc." or "Encl." in the bottom left-hand corner.

"Messrs" should be used only when the title of a firm contains the names of actual persons. When the name of a firm is preceded by the word "The" or a title is included Messrs is never used, e.g.

> Messrs Jones & Brown
> The Longmore Metal Co.
> Sir John Paterson & Co.

It is common practice to use the title Messrs before the name of a limited company but as a limited liability company is really an impersonal body from the legal point of view it should not be preceded by Messrs, although this title is often used if the name of a company contains personal names. It is preferable, when writing to a limited company, to address the communication to an official, e.g. *The Secretary*.

The words "Personal", "Private" or "Confidential" should be typed two spaces above the name of the person to whom the letter is addressed, and underlined.

The words "For the attention of Mr Blank" should be typed two spaces below the name and address of the company, and underlined. Two spaces below that, commence Dear Sirs, not Dear Sir.

Followers are second and subsequent pages of a letter. They should contain name of addressee, page number and date all on one line unless A5 paper is used when the page number can be placed two spaces higher up. This will avoid an over-crowded line. Never take two or three lines to a second page, nor take the last line of a paragraph to the top of a page. It is also considered incorrect to commence a paragraph and type only one line of it at the bottom of a page.

Modern

The most up-to-date way of setting out letters is the fully-blocked method with open punctuation.

"Fully-blocked" means that every line commences at the left-hand margin, i.e. reference, date, inside name and address, salutation, subject heading, paragraphs, complimentary close, signature and designation, with the usual line spacing in between.

A continuation page is typed in the same way with page number, date and name of recipient all commencing at the left hand margin with the same line spacing in between as on the first page.

"Open punctuation" means the omission of *all* punctuation in the date, inside name and address (including omission of full stops after initials), salutation and complimentary close.

In the body of the letter punctuation is omitted for abbreviations, eg, GPO, BEA

With fully-blocked paragraphs type in single-line spacing.

The above layout will be accepted by examining bodies provided the style is consistently used throughout.

2. OFFICIAL LETTERS

Official letters are those sent out by Government Offices. The following points should be noted:

Usually typed in single spacing.

Use a left-hand margin of one inch on A4 paper and half an inch on A5, and leave a right-hand margin of two spaces beyond the longest line.

Continue on back of sheet and reverse the margins.

The address should be typed at the foot of the first page, even when the letter continues to a second or third page, in the "indent" form and placed half an inch back into the margin for A4 paper and a quarter of an inch for A5 paper.

A space is usually provided for the reference which may not be on the same line as the date.

Official letters usually commence SIR, GENTLEMEN or MADAM and the complimentary close is—

I am, Sir,

Your obedient servant,

A catchword is used *only* in official correspondence as under—

As we have received no reply to our letter we

/regret

Enclosures are indicated by a dash in the margin against each line wherein they are mentioned.

Official letters may now be set out in the fully-blocked style. Subject headings are often typed in capital letters with no underscoring.

3. ENVELOPE ADDRESSING

The following are the important points:

Place the address parallel to the length of the envelope.

Commence half-way down to allow room for stamps and post mark.

Secure balance by having approximately equal margins on both sides of the address. The Post Office prefers the address to be typed towards the right-hand side of the envelope.

Type in single-line spacing. The block method is preferable.

Large envelopes may be addressed in double-line spacing unless the address is a long one.

Type each item on a separate line and the town in capitals.

In the majority of places the name of the county is also required.

The postcode should be the last item of information given in an address and it should be typed on a line by itself. The Post Office instructions state: "If it is quite impossible to do this, then a space of at least two characters, preferably six, should be left between the code and whatever precedes it." These instructions, however, apply more to addressograph plates, where space may be limited.

The postcode should always be shown in capitals and no full stops or other punctuation marks should be used between the characters of a code.

The two halves of the code should never be joined together; a clear space equivalent to at least one character should be left between the two parts of the code.

Never underline a code.

The words "Personal", "Urgent", "Confidential", "For the attention of . . ." are typed two spaces above the name of the addressee and underlined.

4. TITLES AND FORMS OF ADDRESS

Title	Form of Address	Salutation	Complimentary Close
Archbishop	His Grace The Lord Archbishop of——	My Lord Archbishop,	I have the honour to be, my Lord Archbishop, Your Lordship's obedient servant,
Baron	The Right Hon. Lord ——	My Lord,	I have the honour to be, my Lord, Your Lordship's obedient servant,
Baroness	The Right Hon. Lady ——	Madam,	I have the honour to be, Madam, Your Ladyship's obedient servant,
Baronet	Sir Robert ——, Bt.	Sir,	I have the honour to be, Sir, Your obedient servant,
Baronet's Wife	Lady ——	Madam,	I have the honour to be, Madam, Your obedient servant,
Bishop	The Right Rev. The Lord Bishop of——	My Lord Bishop,	I have the honour to be, my Lord, Your Lordship's obedient servant
Countess	The Right Hon. The Countess of——	Madam,	I have the honour to be, Madam, Your Ladyship's obedient servant,
Duchess	Her Grace The Duchess of——	Madam,	I am, Madam, Your Grace's most obedient servant,
Duke	His Grace The Duke of——	My Lord Duke,	I am, my Lord Duke, Your Grace's most obedient servant,
Earl	The Right Hon. The Earl of——	My Lord,	I have the honour to be, my Lord, Your Lordship's obedient servant,
Knight	Sir John ——	Sir,	I am, Sir, Your obedient servant,
Knight's Wife	Lady ——	Madam,	I am, Madam, Your obedient servant,

Lord Mayor	The Right Worshipful The Lord Mayor of ——	My Lord Mayor,	I am, my Lord Mayor, Your obedient servant,
Lord Provost	The Lord Provost of ——	My Lord Provost,	I am, my Lord Provost, Your obedient servant,
Marchioness	The Most Hon. The Marchioness of ——	Madam,	I have the honour to be, Madam, Your Ladyship's obedient servant,
Marquess	The Most Hon. The Marquess of ——	My Lord,	I have the honour to be, my Lord, Your Lordship's obedient servant,
Mayor	The Right Worshipful The Mayor of ——	Sir,	I am, Sir, Your obedient servant,
Minister of Church	The Rev. —. —.	Reverend Sir,	I am, Reverend Sir, Your obedient servant,
Viscount	The Right Hon. The Viscount ——	My Lord,	I have the honour to be, my Lord, Your Lordship's obedient servant,
Viscountess	The Right Hon. The Viscountess ——	Madam,	I have the honour to be, Madam, Your Ladyship's obedient servant,

Distinctions gained are typed after a person's name in the following order:

1. Decorations and Honours, e.g. V.C., D.S.O., K.B.E., O.B.E.,
2. Educational Qualifications, e.g. M.A., B.Com.
3. Member of Parliament or Justice of the Peace, e.g. M.P., J.P.

    Examples: O.B.E., M.A., J.P.   V.C., B.Com., M.P.

N.B. The abbreviation V.C. takes precedence over all other decorations and honours and a higher rank in an order always includes the lower. Certain initials are invariably given after a person's name (e.g. V.C., K.G. and O.M.) but the less important ones can be omitted. *Jun.* is always typed before Esq.

CHAPTER VII

1. Carbon Copying
2. Press Copying
3. Stencil Cutting
4. Spirit Duplicating
5. Offset Litho Duplicating

1. CARBON COPYING

Manifolding is another name for carbon copying.
The most important points in carbon copying are:

1. The type must be in good condition to get clear impressions.
2. The type must be kept very clean, especially the letters e, s, a, w, m and n.
3. The platen of the machine should be fairly hard if a large number of copies is required; it must also be kept free from ridges.
4. A backing sheet is an advantage, especially for single copies.
5. Any unevenness in depressing the keys will show more on the carbon copies than on the top copy. M and W, capitals and fractions should be struck more heavily and punctuation marks more lightly. Use a sharp touch throughout.

Single carbon paper has the coating pigment on one side only and double carbons are coated on both sides. Using very thin paper and single coated carbons (the kind in general use) about eight copies may be taken. Specially thin, practically transparent, paper and double carbons may be used if a large number of copies is required, up to about 20. It may also be desirable to disengage the ribbon and type direct on the top sheet. Each sheet of carbon produces a copy in reverse on the paper above and a normal copy on the paper below. The reverse copy is read through the paper. Two sheets of copy paper are required to each carbon.

Carbons may be obtained in different colours—Purple, Black, Blue, Red, Green and Brown.

1. in order to match the ribbon,
2. so as to produce a different colour for different departments, or
3. to draw attention to some item.

If a note has to be typed on a carbon copy and is not required on the original insert a small piece of paper at the printing point between ribbon and paper.

If the note has to be typed on the original and is not to appear on the carbon insert a piece of paper behind carbon.

When correcting carbon copies separately insert a small piece of carbon between the ribbon and paper to secure uniformity in appearance of carbon copies.

Carbon copying is used extensively in "billing", the term used to cover the system of typing, at one operation, the invoice, the entry in the Day Book and as many carbon copies as are required. In this instance it may be necessary to omit certain information from some of the copies. The carbons are cut in different sizes to get this result.

Carbons should be kept flat and not allowed to crease. The "treed" effect produced by carbons is caused by creasing. They must also be handled lightly and kept away from heat. If cheap varieties are used they give blurred and uneven copies. Turn them upside down frequently or cut a strip off the top to make sure they are as evenly worn as possible.

Difficulty is often experienced in inserting carbons straight and quickly between sheets of paper especially if a large number of copies is required. A good method is to insert the sheets of paper into the typewriter without the carbons, grip them for about half an inch, bring the sheets of paper forward and turning them back separately insert a sheet of carbon between, carbon side forward. This will also facilitate removal of the carbons. Hold the top edges of paper in one hand and pull the bottom edges of the carbons out with the other hand in one operation.

3. PRESS COPYING

Letters can be press copied as an alternative to taking carbon copies. Used mainly in legal offices. They must, however, be typed with a copying ribbon. The advantages of this method over carbon copying are that any corrections made on the original, after removal from the machine, appear on the copy and the signature to the letter, which should be written with copying ink, appears also. If carbons are used corrections may be omitted unless the operator remembers, and the signature never appears. There are two ways of taking press copies:
1. By letter book, damping sheets and press.
2. By letter copier machine with chemically prepared paper.

3. STENCIL CUTTING

Typewriter requirements:
  Good sharp type which must be clean.
  Hard cylinder.
  If cylinder is soft use additional hard backing sheet.

Directions:

  1. Thoroughly clean type.
  2. Throw ribbon out of gear by means of stencil switch.
  3. Insert stencil with back of backing sheet next to cylinder.
  4. Type with a definite sharp touch in order to cut the stencil clearly.
  5. Use correcting fluid for mistakes.

A stencil is made of a special composition which is cut through by the keys striking directly on to it. Punctuation marks, thin letters and the letter "o" will need to be struck more lightly. Letters having a large surface, capitals and fractions will need to be struck more heavily. Uneven key depression will result in uneven appearance when the work is rolled off.

If the middle of a letter is punched out replace it with a pin or with a moistened finger. Errors can be rectified by using correcting fluid and retyping, or "grafting" with a piece of material cut from another stencil. This is done by cutting out the part of the stencil containing the wrong words and replacing with part of another stencil on which the correct words have been typed. The edges of the patch must overlap the space and it should be fixed to the inner side of the stencil by using correcting fluid.

If cracks appear during the rolling off lift stencil and stretch more tightly over machine or cover cracks with gummed paper or obliterating fluid.

Ruling on a stencil can be done by the underscore, a ruler and a sharp penknife or a stylus. A stylus is used for the signature.

Special absorbent paper is required for running off. If non-absorbent paper is used a sheet of blotting paper must be placed between the sheets to prevent "offsetting", i.e. the ink being transferred from one sheet to another, unless an electro-spray is attached to the duplicating machine. This sprays a fine powder on to each sheet thereby preventing offsetting.

For checking purposes a carbon copy may be taken when typing the stencil. This is known as a "proof" copy.

Keep standing is the term used for stencils which are laid aside for further use.

4. SPIRIT DUPLICATING

In this process spirit is used as the duplicating medium.

Special paper, often highly glazed on one side, and special carbons, called Transfer Sheets, are required. The master or original copy is prepared by placing a sheet of the special carbon behind the typing paper—glazed side of paper to carbonized side of carbon—and typing normally through the ribbon on to the front surface of the paper. This gives a mirror impression on the reverse side of the paper as the carbon is transferred on to it.

Carbons can be obtained in seven colours, black, blue, purple, red, green, brown and yellow and it is possible by removing one colour of carbon and using another colour, or, while the work is still in the typewriter, inserting another piece of carbon of a different colour on top of the original to have a variety of colours on the one master.

It is, however, not possible to erase as in ordinary typing. The carbon must be scraped off the back—an ordinary penknife is suitable. A new piece of carbon is placed behind the scraped off letter, and the correct letter typed in.

When the master copy is fitted on to the duplicating machine it is from the mirror impression on the reverse side that the copies are obtained.

5. OFFSET LITHO DUPLICATING

This is actually a form of printing. The master is either a metal or paper plate. Metal plates may have to be prepared by an outside firm, but the paper plates can be prepared on a typewriter using an "offset litho" ribbon. As the underlying principle here is that water and grease will not mix, the ribbon contains "grease".

Type must be clean and the keys struck with a firm, even touch to give a clear impression. To make corrections an offset eraser should be used applying medium pressure to remove the greasy part of the image. A faint impression can be left rather than damage the plate by too hard rubbing. Retype using the same pressure. Handle the plates by their ends so that no grease or dirt is transferred from your hands.

Any quality of copy paper can be used for the copies, and this method is useful for preparing letter headings, invoices, price lists and magazines. It gives a better finish than ink duplicating and is cheaper than using the services of a printer.

CHAPTER VIII

1. INVOICING

Invoices are usually typewritten on special headed forms and may be typed in single or double spacing as required.

They are composed of:

1. The items, giving length, quantity or weight, and description of goods.
2. The rate per yard, pound, dozen, etc.
3. The calculations and total amount charged.

Carbon copies are taken.

Tabular stops are used.

Variable line spacer may be required for date and customer's name if lines are to be typed on.

Back spacer used for an odd long line.

The £ sign is typed above units of pounds unless the pounds run into a large number, in which case the £ sign appears over the middle.

When typing pounds and pence place the £ sign above the decimal point.

Rate column generally typed to end two spaces to the left of the £ sign in front of total, i.e. the longest line of figures, unless a column is provided.

A double line is drawn beneath the total.

Debit and Credit Notes are typed similarly. Credit Notes are usually typed in red for distinction.

2. SPECIFICATIONS

A specification is a statement of particulars and a description of the work to be done by builders, plumbers, electricians, house decorators and engineers. It consists of three parts:

1. The heading
2. The body
3. The side headings

Specifications are usually typed on foolscap or A4 paper with a record ribbon; carbon copies are taken. Short specifications are typed in double spacing, long specifications in single spacing with double spacing between paragraphs. They are endorsed in the same way as legal documents.

The heading or introductory part is always typed in double spacing commencing at 30° with the word "Specification" in spaced capitals and the subsequent lines are indented to 35°. If an architect's name is included this comes immediately after the heading commencing about 45° or according to the length of the line—each line of the address being indented five spaces and typed in single spacing.

The date comes next commencing at 25°.

The body has a margin of 25°.

The side headings are always typed in block capitals, in single spacing if they consist of more than one line, and with a margin of 10°.

If there are sub-headings they are centred in spaced or unspaced capitals, underlined or not.

If a specification consists of a heading only, i.e. no introductory paragraph, this can be typed in displayed capitals, in double spacing and centred between 25° and right-hand margin.

3. BALANCE SHEETS

Balance Sheets can be typed in the following ways according to the number of items or size of typewriter:

1. On a single sheet of quarto, A4 or foolscap paper.
2. On a sheet of foolscap or A4 paper folded in half so that each side measures $6\frac{1}{2}''$ or 6″ in width.
3. On two sheets of any size of paper joined neatly together after typing.
4. On draft or brief paper.

If typing on a single sheet of quarto, A4 or foolscap paper type alternate sides until one side is completed, then continue with the other and type both totals on the same level. Each side should occupy exactly half the width of the paper and the main heading should be centred over the width of the paper. Outside margins should be equal.

The same rules apply when typing on draft or brief paper.

If typing on two sheets of paper take care that the respective sides correspond. The heading must run across both sheets. The side containing the larger number of items should be typed first and the second sheet must be marked with a pencil so that the heading, the first item and the totals will be on the same level when the two sheets are placed together. There must be narrow and equal margins on the right side of the liabilities sheet and on the left side of the assets sheet. The left margin on the liabilities side and the right margin on the assets side must be equal.

The same care must be taken when typing on a sheet of folded paper.

Leader dots can be inserted if necessary.

4. MEMOS

Memorandum forms or "memos" as they are briefly called are quite often given in examinations. Printed forms are usually provided. As these forms are used for internal communications or between branch and head office they do not have any salutation or complimentary close. The printed forms can vary in layout and may include dotted lines in the heading for completion. Type just above the dots—not on them.

CHAPTER IX

1. LEGAL WORK

Black record ribbon is required because it will not fade.

Use a "brief" machine if possible.

Various sizes of paper are used.

No erasures must ever occur in an engrossment.

Punctuation marks, except at the end of a clause, are left out as it is possible for them to convey a double meaning.

All abbreviations must be typed in full.

All figures, except house numbers, must be typed in words in the engrossment.

Blank spaces at the end of a line should be filled in with hyphens to prevent words being added.

A draft is typed first in treble spacing with wide left-hand margin in order that alterations and additions may be written in easily. Figures, sums of money and dates need not be spelt out but other abbreviations should be typed in full. The word "draft" must appear on the endorsement.

A clean draft is usually typed next in double spacing. Figures, etc., need not yet be spelt out. As it is still a draft the word "draft" appears on the endorsement.

The engrossment is finally typed, for signature by the client. Double sheets of draft or brief paper are used, and it is typed in double spacing on both sides of the paper. There should be no abbreviations or erasures. Figures, sums of money and dates are typed in words. A margin occupying a quarter of the width of the paper is left on the left-hand side of the first and every odd-numbered page but no margin is left on the right-hand side. On the even-numbered pages a similar margin is left on the left-hand side but there is also a margin of about 5° on the right-hand side. This is called the "stitching margin" to allow the document to be sewn together after typing, with no words hidden. The last outside page is always left blank for the endorsement. Capitalization is made use of in order to make certain portions stand out: the name of the document and the word "between" in spaced capitals, the names of the parties when first mentioned and the first word or words of each clause in unspaced capitals.

Pages are numbered at the foot for English Documents and at the top full out (e.g. Page Three) for Scottish Documents.

In English legal documents the deed is completed by typing the Testimonium Clause and Attestation Clause. These vary but the following is an example:

IN WITNESS whereof I have hereunto set my hand this .....(Date)... day of .....(Month)... One thousand nine hundred and .....(Year)... before the witnesses hereto subscribing.

SIGNED SEALED AND DELIVERED)
by the above-named .....(Name)... in the)
presence of)

In Scottish legal documents the two are combined in one clause called the Testing Clause. This clause varies according to the number of parties signing but a simple example follows:

IN WITNESS whereof these presents typewritten on this and the .....(No.)... preceding pages are subscribed by me .....(Name)... at .....(Place)... on the .....(Date)... day of .....(Month)... Nineteen hundred and .....(Year)... before these witnesses .....(Name)... , ...(Designation)... , ...(Address)... and .....(Name)... , ...(Designation)... , ...(Address)...

When a copy is made the word *copy* should precede the name of the deed on the endorsement and the word *signed* should be placed before the typed signature to the document.

The endorsement should contain date, names of parties, brief description of contents and name of solicitor.

Foolscap or A4 documents are folded in two from left to right and the endorsement is typed on the side then uppermost.

Larger documents are folded into four from bottom to top and the endorsement is typed on the section then uppermost.

2. DISPLAYED MATTER

Displayed work may consist of Menus, Advertisements, Hand Bills, Reports, Agendas, Minutes and Tabulated Statements.

In typewriting "displayed" means the artistic arrangement of headings, sub-headings and other matter. All headings should be centred and balanced with one another, the idea being to distribute the matter effectively over the page, setting out principal items prominently. Patience is required in making calculations and skill is needed in the use of capitals, spaced capitals, small letters, underscoring, the variation of line spacing and the employment of white space. The period should never be placed at the line end of headings. The principal item should be typed in capitals to give it greater prominence. If spaced capitals are used they are more easy to read when underlined. Sub-titles are better typed in small letters with the initial letter of each important word capitalized. Small words such as "and" naturally have no initial capital.

The study of magazines or newspapers will act as a good guide as to how the printer sets out advertisements, although, of course, he has a greater variety of type to work with.

Spacing for Headings

Between words of unspaced small letters		I
„ „ of unspaced capital letters		I or 2
„ „ of single-spaced small or capital letters		3

Display work in examinations is moving away from the old method of copying a piece of work exactly as it is given. The new trend is to encourage thinking and rearrangement of work, as would be expected in an office, and a very much wider range of documents is now being set involving a more thorough knowledge of theory than has been required in the past.

The instructions at the top of each exercise must be read *very, very* carefully. Even the addition of an "s" can make a difference—e.g. leave margin*s* of $1\frac{1}{2}$ inches. These directions may also, as well as stating how the document should be set out, contain information which has to be incorporated in the typing. The instructions, however, are not always complete at the top of the page. Look to see if there are more hand-written instructions in the margins or at the foot of the page. These additional notes usually carry an indication that they are for the "Typist".

The following points, with notes, are given as an indication of the type of instructions now being set.

Type on half a sheet of paper.	The paper can be used either way according to the length of the exercise.
Use A4 paper lengthwise.	If a long carriage machine is not available A4 paper will require to be folded.
Type a menu, programme or play on folded paper.	If the width and length are not known measure the paper with a ruler, remembering—10/12 letters to the inch across, 6 lines to the inch down.
Arrange and complete application forms.	This often necessitates lines of dots. Leave a space before commencing dots and use double-line spacing. When completing the form, type just above the dots—*not on them.*
Type a form in duplicate and complete duplicate *only* from given information.	This may require lines of dots or straight lines. Make sure there is sufficient space left for completion.
Copy a diagram.	This may not be as difficult as it appears to be. Study it carefully before beginning to type.
Leave blank space/s of so many inches down for later insertion of diagram/s.	Remember six lines to the inch and type on the following line.
Set out documents in *correct* style—programmes, plays, poems, memos, agendas, minutes, specifications and legal work.	Here theory must be known, especially the different margins and line spacing.
Type a balance sheet on two A4 pages, or on A4 paper lengthwise.	If a long carriage machine is not available A4 paper will require to be folded and the longer side typed first.
Change a letter to a circular letter.	Care is required in leaving sufficient lines for inside name and address. It is better to err on the generous side.
Type a letter from given information.	Make sure all the information is incorporated. Score out each part after it has been typed.
Type a letter with a continuation page.	Particulars for second sheet are—name *only*, page number and date all in one line. See also p. 26.

Type a letter on A5 paper.

As a rule the paper is used vertically and margins set according to the length of the letter. As little as half-inch margins can be left, if necessary.

Take more than one carbon copy and direct copies to given departments or people.

There are various ways of directing copies. The most common way is to type on the original at the bottom— Copy to: and list the people/departments, underlining or ticking a different name on each copy.

Envelope/postcard addressing.

See page 27.

Check calculations in letter, report or tabulated statement.

Check carefully where indicated.

Change type of paragraphs.

See page 19.

Rearrange work in
—alphabetical order
—numerical order, commencing with lowest or highest number
—alphabetical/geographical order
—price order, commencing with lowest or highest price.
—date order

As this type of work is growing in importance, get as much practice as possible in rearranging all types of lists. Quite often the list requires to be arranged in two ways, e.g. names alphabetically arranged under towns also alphabetically arranged. It might be a help to jot down a few notes on a piece of paper to get a clearer view, or, if possible, mark down the side of the exam paper in pencil the required order. Then count the items given and your marking as a check that each item has been accounted for. Score out each part after it has been typed. In some cases it may only be possible to mark in groups and to type each group after it has been marked.

Transfer columns in tabular statement.

Keep firmly fixed in your mind what is required.

Extract information and set out as a tab. statement.

Read instructions very carefully then underline on the examination paper the *exact* information asked for.

Prepare a table from given information.

Read instructions thoroughly. An indication of headings is usually given.

Add extra column/s to tabular statement from given information.

The headings to the columns may have to be abbreviated.

Insert or omit leader dots, commas or ruling.

Mark on the examination paper, in pencil, what is required.

Type tabular statement with certain portions omitted but leaving sufficient space for omitted parts.

When calculating space to be left for omitted lines, remember one more line space has to be turned up; e.g. if 12 line spaces have to be left, type on 13th line.

Type top headings of tab. vertically or at an angle.

Six line spaces down make an inch in which 10 pica characters can be typed. Therefore count the letter spaces required and turn this into line spaces. Rather leave too much than too little. When calculating the statement across, the width of the longest line in each column must be compared with the width of the vertical heading to find out which will take up more space; e.g. six spaces across will require a little more space than a heading of three lines up, therefore six spaces is the width of that column. Again, if a heading is six lines in width—1 inch that will allow up to 10 characters to be typed in width below. If there are more than 10 characters, take this number as width; if less, take 10 characters as width.

3. MANUSCRIPT REPORTS, etc.

Copying from manuscript is a very important part of all typewriting examinations. The following points should be noted:

Read the instructions carefully at the head of each exercise, particularly the instructions as to depth of line spacing required.

Note that catchwords, P.T.O., etc., are never used.

It is preferable to read the whole of the matter through before commencing but if time is short read a portion to become familiar with the subject matter and handwriting.

All abbreviations must be typed in full except the recognized commercial abbreviations such as f.o.b., etc.

Headings and sub-headings must be centred over line of typing. They may be single underlined but *never* double or treble- underlined. No full stop after headings.

See Displayed Work for letter spacing of headings. For spacing between heading and body of work use double line spacing if text is in single line spacing; if in double line spacing use treble line spacing.

Be consistent in lay out, especially underlining and measurements.

Correct all typing mistakes and do not omit any portion. Make sure that the capital I is used for Roman Numerals.

The first page should not be numbered but the following pages should be numbered at the *top*.

See if there is a "Note to typist" and follow instructions. It is only a note for guidance and of course the words are not typed in.

Indicate by a pencil line at bottom of paper where last line is to be typed— an inch from the bottom.

Never type just one line of a paragraph at the foot of a page nor take a final line to the top of a second page.

Any insets, e.g. paragraphs commencing (a), (b), etc., are always typed in single spacing and indented equally from *each* margin, i.e. the lines finish as many spaces from the right-hand margin as they were indented from the left. Roman numerals commencing paragraphs are typed with their right-hand edge even— (i)   (I)

        (ii)   (II)

        (iii)   (III)

Names, numbers and sums of money are never divided at line ends.

A footnote must always be typed in single spacing at the foot of the page to which it refers, usually indented five spaces. A line or portion of a line is typed across the page before the footnote commences. As a footnote cannot be split sufficient space must be left to get it all in. Footnote signs, ✻ ‡ ‡ or a number must always be raised half a space in body of text and in actual footnote. This sign must be typed close to the word to which it refers in the text, but in the footnote one space should separate the sign from the word following.

If the following words occur and are meant to be used in the abbreviated form always leave a space between figure and word: in., ft., oz. and lb., e.g. 1 *in.*, 2 *ft.*, 3 *oz.* and 1 *lb.*

If sloping fractions occur and are used with whole numbers it is necessary to leave one space between the whole number and the fraction, e.g. 31 4/5ths. When the fraction is provided on the keyboard a space is not necessary, e.g. 4⅜.

If Circulars, Time Sheets, Memoranda, Appendices, Reference Lists or any unknown matter are included as part of the manuscript work use the copy as a guide. There is often no set way of typing these but as long as the work is accurate and clearly presented no difficulty should be experienced. In such documents as appendices, reference lists and similar matter where a great many of the words are abbreviated keep the abbreviations, e.g. *Ed. for Edition, Vol. for Volume, p. for page, Hyg. for Hygiene, Sc. for Scene, etc.* as it is impossible to know all technical contractions.

5. TABULAR STATEMENTS

Tabular work means the display of statistical information in two or more columns. The work must be planned out before beginning to type. It should be centred vertically and horizontally, compact but not overcrowded. All headings and each line in a heading must be centred equally one with the other. The margins must be equal, blank paper at top and bottom equal and the width between the columns must be the same. When the statement is finally ruled this can be done entirely in ink, or by use of the underscore, or by a mixture of both methods. If no outside lines are shown in the examination paper this is left to the candidate's discretion. No double underlining is ever used except for totals.

If the lines are being drawn entirely by ink to make sure they will be straight draw them lightly in pencil before work is withdrawn from machine. An odd number of spaces between columns is necessary if this method is being used. For vertical lines bring the nick in the alignment scale along to the correct place for the line, release the platen and turn it by means of the cylinder knob while holding the pencil point firmly in the nick. For horizontal lines, place the point of the pencil again in the nick and draw carriage along. The lines can be gone over in ink afterwards. Another method is to put dots in stencil at the appropriate places and join afterwards.

When calculating the layout of a statement the widest item in a column may be in the heading or the total. One space is usually allowed for each vertical line and one space at each side but in a very wide statement it is often not possible to leave as many as three spaces between columns. Judgment must be used here. If the total of the columns and spaces between is too high and does not leave sufficient spaces for reasonable margins reduce width of descriptive column by running single lines into two lines. In the descriptive column second and subsequent lines of an item are indented. No abbreviations are allowed, e.g. "&" for "and", except perhaps in a column heading where the name of a month is often abbreviated.

When typing tabular statements type across the paper line by line, not down column by column. Leader dots are usually inserted in the subject column and they can be typed as follows: two dots and three spaces, three dots and two spaces, regularly spaced single dots or a continuous line of dots. The dots must be typed underneath one another but must not run into the word they connect. There should be at least one space between the end of a word and the commencement of the dots, and no typing line should extend beyond leaders. A stop can be set for either the longest line in a column and the space bar used for shorter lines or the stop set for where the majority of the lines commence and the back-spacer and space bar used for longer or shorter lines.

Type footnotes in single spacing and raise the footnote signs half a space in text and in actual footnote. In the text the footnote sign must be typed close to the word to which it refers, but in the actual footnote one space should separate the sign from the word following.

Finally always check the width of the paper before commencing because it could be a degree wider and this would have to be allowed for in making calculations.

CHAPTER X

1. Agendas
2. Minutes

1. AGENDAS

An Agenda is a list of items to be discussed at a business meeting, and arranged in the order in which they are to be dealt with. Foolscap or A4 paper is used and they can be typed in two ways:

1. Across the width of the paper with a 1½ inch margin.
2. Down the left-hand side of the paper with a half-inch margin leaving the right-hand portion blank for the Chairman's remarks.

The heading giving the name of the company, type of meeting, place, date and time of meeting should be centred and displayed effectively; the word "Agenda" usually in spaced capitals and centred. Each item is numbered and typed in single spacing with double between items. Sub-sections are indented, numbered in a different manner and typed in single spacing. Example of heading follows:

THE NORTHERN ESTATE COMPANY LTD

ANNUAL GENERAL MEETING
to be held at the Registered Office of the Company
on Tuesday, 4th July, 1972
at 11 a.m.

A G E N D A

2. MINUTES

Minutes are an official record of proceedings of a meeting arranged in the order in which they were discussed and usually following the order in which they appeared in the Agenda. Foolscap or A4 paper is used and they are typed across the width of the paper with a generous left-hand margin in which may be placed side headings.

The heading gives practically the same details as an Agenda heading and can be either displayed, or typed from the centre of the paper to the right-hand margin in single spacing as a hanging paragraph. A list of the members present indicating who was Chairman, etc., is typed next in single spacing and centred. Below that comes a list of apologies for absence in single spacing. The body follows typed in double spacing. Examples of headings:

MINUTES of ANNUAL GENERAL MEETING
of THE NORTHERN ESTATE COMPANY LTD
held at the Registered Office of the Company on
Tuesday, 4th July, 1972, at 11 a.m.

THE NORTHERN ESTATE COMPANY LTD.

MINUTES of ANNUAL GENERAL MEETING
held at the Registered Office of the Company
on Tuesday, 4th July, 1972, at 11 a.m.

CHAPTER XI

1. Literary Work
   (Authors' Manuscripts, etc.)
2. Plays
3. Programmes
4. Poetry

1. LITERARY WORK

Literary work means the typing of stories, articles or lectures. These are typed on quarto or A4 paper, on one side only, in double spacing leaving a margin of 15°. Short quotations or extracts consisting of a few words or a few lines are typed along with the text but long quotations or extracts are typed in single spacing and indented. When preparing work for the printer a footnote should be typed in single spacing in the next line immediately following the word to which it refers and a line drawn across the page before and after the footnote. A raised asterisk, etc. is placed after and above the word to which the footnote refers and immediately in front of the relative footnote. If a word has to appear in italics when printed it should be underlined. Headings, including chapter headings of books, are typed in capitals in the centre and further down the page than the normal line of typing. All pages, except the first, are numbered at the top in the centre, and the numbers should follow consecutively from the beginning to the end of the book irrespective of the division of the book into chapters. Arabic figures are used for page numbering and large Roman Numerals for chapter headings. A preface should be paged in small Roman Numerals.

When typing a book manuscript set out first of all title page, list of contents and list of illustrations.

2. PLAYS

Plays can be divided into two parts:

General copies containing the complete play.
Separate actors' parts with cues.

The complete play is typed in single spacing with double between the parts. Quarto or A4 paper is used and a black or black and red record ribbon. The description of the Scene, if a long one, is typed as a hanging paragraph commencing at 25°, indenting subsequent lines to 30°. The first word SCENE is typed in capitals. The main portion starts at 20° indenting each first line and the characters are placed in the margin at 10° and typed in capitals. Short stage directions are placed in the centre of the page and enclosed in brackets, but if they consist of one word only type, in brackets, along with the speech. Lengthy stage directions begin at the margin with second and subsequent lines indented a few spaces. All stage directions are either typed in red or underlined in red to show that they are not spoken words. All words not spoken, including the description of the scene, are typed or underlined in red. The first four pages of a play are as follows:

Page 1 Title Page (Gives name, type, number of acts and name of author, each on a separate line, displayed and typed in capitals)

Page 2 Synopsis of Acts and Scenery (Heading in capitals, each Act and Scene occupies a separate line and these lines are displayed down centre of page)

Page 3 List of Characters and Cast (Set out in two columns—Characters can be typed in small letters underlined or capital letters with no underlining)

Page 4 List of Costumes (Set out in two columns)

An actor's part contains the words spoken by one particular character and need only be headed with that character's name typed in capitals in the centre beneath the title of the play. Typed on octavo or A5 paper in double line spacing with a 5° margin. The cues, which are the last few words spoken by the previous character, are preceded by a few dots and should contain a guiding word. They are always typed on a separate line, the dots beginning at the margin. Cues, being unspoken words, are typed or underlined in red. Any stage directions are enclosed in brackets and also typed or underlined in red.

3. PROGRAMMES

When setting out a Concert Programme there should be equal margins at each side and equal blank space top and bottom. The right-hand margin should be kept even. The name of the artist and description of item should be in capitals. The name of the item should appear in inverted commas, and the name of the

composer should be underscored, so that it will be printed in italics. An example
follows:

WALTZ "The Emperor"   MISS MARGARET ELLIOT   Strauss
SELECTION "Show Boat"   MR GEORGE BAYNE   Jerome Kern

An ornamental border can be placed round a programme.

4. POETRY

There are certain rules to follow in typing poetry so as to give the work a
well-balanced effect. Single line spacing is used with equal margins, two or
three lines are left between verses, and every line starts with a capital letter.
The rules are as follows:

1. The title is typed in capitals.
2. The author's name is placed at the end, preceded by a dash, in brackets
   or underscored and lining up roughly with longest line.
3. Where there is no rhyme or when the successive lines rhyme there is no
   indentation.
4. When alternate lines rhyme the first, third and fifth lines begin at the
   margin and the second, fourth, sixth, etc., lines are indented two or
   three spaces.
5. If some lines are very short in length indentation may have to be more
   than two or three spaces in order to maintain balance.

Hook-in is a term used mainly in the typing of poetry. If there are too many
words in a line in comparison with the other lines the extra words are placed
above or below their own line. See example under Literary Definitions.

CHAPTER XII

QUESTIONS AND ANSWERS

1. Q. How is a typewriter kept in good working order?
   A. Keep covered when not in use.
   Clean lightly every morning.
   Clean thoroughly once a week.
   Oil carriage runways occasionally, using only a drop or two of typewriter oil.

2. Q. Why is a backing sheet used?
   A. A backing sheet is used to prevent injury to the cylinder through hard typing; it gives a better finish to work which is done on thin paper, and also deadens the sound a little.

3. Q. What is the advantage of a copyholder?
   A. A copyholder brings the matter up to the level of the eyes and saves straining.

4. Q. What are lower and upper case characters?
   A. Lower case characters are those typed without depressing the shift key and include small letters and figures. Upper case characters are those typed whilst the shift key is depressed and include capital letters.

5. Q. What are superior and inferior characters?
   A. Superior characters are those placed above the normal line of typing and inferior characters are those placed below the normal line of typing, e.g. $c^3 \times b^2$, H_2O, N_2

6. Q. What are sloping fractions?
   A. Sloping fractions are fractions using the oblique sign, e.g. 4/5ths.

7. Q. What is a "dead" key?
   A. A "dead" key is one which when depressed does not cause the carriage to move forward the usual space. It is used for accents and is struck before the character which is to appear underneath.

8. Q. What is the difference between a dash and a hyphen?

A. A dash separates clauses and there is a space before and after. A hyphen divides compound words or words into syllables and there is no space before or after.

9. Q. What are the uses of the back-spacer?

A. The back-spacer can be used to retype a light character, for half-space correcting, for combination signs, in tabular work, and back-spacing for a short heading.

10. Q. What is the difference between the margin release key and the line lock release key?

A. The only difference between the margin release and the line lock release is that the line lock release acts only on the right-hand margin while the margin release can release both margins. They are frequently called 'margin release' for both margins.

11. Q. What are the uses of the variable line spacer?

A. The variable line spacer is used—
    (a) for typing on ruled lines;
    (b) for typing double lines under a total;
    (c) when it is necessary to raise or lower characters; and
    (d) to obtain the original typing line in order to make a correction.

12. Q. Describe the functions of the paper release lever.

A. The functions of the paper release lever are to straighten the paper should it have been inserted obliquely, to allow the paper to be adjusted when re-inserted for correction of errors and for withdrawal when a page is complete.

13. Q. When double figures are typed in words how should they be typed?

A. Double figures are typed with a hyphen between, e.g. thirty-four.

14. Q. What is meant by "alignment"?

A. Alignment means the typing of the characters in a straight line, with the tops and bottoms level with each other.

15. Q. What operator's faults cause (a) irregular line spacing?
                                   (b) irregular left-hand margin?

A. Irregular line spacing may be caused by faulty manipulation of the carriage return lever, by using the cylinder knobs to turn up the paper, or by having the line space indicator at single spacing and trusting to memory to turn up two spaces.

Irregular left-hand margin may be caused by not returning the carriage until it comes into contact with the margin stop.

16. Q. How can characters be raised or lowered? Give examples:

A. Characters can be raised or lowered by using the variable line spacer or the platen release lever. Examples 50°, H_2SO_4

17. Q. What are followers?

A. Followers are second and subsequent pages of any typewritten work.

18. Q. To fill in form letters would you use a black or red ribbon?

A. When filling in form letters a red ribbon is better because black matching is often difficult.

19. Q. When an addition or alteration is to be made to a sheet of a document consisting of several sheets fastened together at the top how is the sheet inserted into the machine without unfastening?

A. When a document is fastened together and an alteration is necessary the method of correction is known as "feeding paper backwards" or "backward feed". Insert a sheet of plain paper in the ordinary way and bring it forward above the line indicator at the front of the machine, insert the bottom edge of the sheet to be corrected between the paper in the machine and the cylinder and turn the cylinder backwards, remove the extra sheet of paper from back of machine and adjust the sheet to be corrected.

20. Q. What is a Letter Register?

A. A Letter Register is a book which contains copies of all letters sent out by a business firm, with an index at the beginning.

21. Q. What is a Letter Reference?

A. A Letter Reference may consist of letters or figures or both placed at the top left-hand corner of a letter for future reference to correspondence on the same subject. The usual form is dictator's and typist's initials but it can vary according to the practice of the firm.

22. Q. What does "heavy" or "stiff" and "open" or "easy" mean when referring to punctuation?

A. A passage with a large number of punctuation marks is "heavy" or "stiff" and with only a few "open" or "easy".

23. Q. What is a brace?

A. A brace is a succession of brackets, one below the other, used to link lines together, and the Attestation Clause in legal documents.

24. Q. What is meant by the term "pitch"?

A. Pitch refers to the spacing of the typewriter, i.e., the space occupied by a single character. With elite type the pitch is 12 characters to the inch; with pica 10 characters to the inch.

25. Q. How should a postcode be typed?

A. Use capital letters and figures with no punctuation, e.g. EH4 2JZ

26. Q. What letter is used for the "cypher" or "nought" and what letter for "one" if not provided on the keyboard?

A. The capital "O" is used for the "cypher" and small "el" for "one" in Arabic figures.

27. Q. What are leader dots?

A. Leader dots are successive groups of dots inserted to carry the eye from one point to another, typed in groups of 2 dots 3 spaces, 3 dots 2 spaces, or 1 dot 4 spaces.

28. Q. What is meant by reference marks? Give examples.

A. Reference marks are the signs employed for indicating footnotes, ✳ ‡ ‡

29. Q. What does double and treble underlining beneath a word mean?

A. Double underlining means the word has to be typed in capital letters; treble underlining that the word has to be typed in spaced capital letters.

30. Q. How would you rectify imperfect feeding of the paper when caused through the shiny condition of the cylinder or feed rolls?

A. To rectify imperfect feeding rub the cylinder and feed rolls with benzine or, if this is not sufficient, rub the surface with very fine emery paper.

31. Q. How would you test the paper feed for accuracy in backward and forward travel?

A. To test the paper feed for accuracy in backward and forward travel type a few words, turn the cylinder backwards and forwards, then type over the words again. If there is no sign of a double impression the paper feed is accurate.

32. Q. How is accurate registration secured when re-inserting a typescript into the machine to make a correction?

A. Accurate registration is secured by bringing a thin letter exactly opposite the printing point then using the variable line spacer to get the typing level with the line indicator. Switch the ribbon over to stencil and type the first letter to see if the position is correct.

33. Q. Is there any method of ruling unbroken vertical lines by the typewriter without removing the work from the machine?

A. Unbroken vertical lines can be ruled while work is in the machine by means of a pencil. Place the pencil point in the nick provided in the alignment scale, release the platen and turn it by means of the cylinder knob while holding the pencil firmly.

34. Q. When typing a quotation how would you indicate the omission of a few words from the beginning, middle or end of the quoted passage?

A. Type three spaced dots at the beginning and in the middle but four at the end to include the full stop.

35. Q. What depth of line spacing is used for tabular matter in the body of a business letter? Give a reason for your answer.

A. Tabular work is typed in single line spacing in order to make that portion stand out clearly from the rest of the work.

36. Q. State the various uses of the tabular key.

A. The tabular key can be used for columns in tabular work, for the date, paragraphs and subscription to a letter, and in invoicing.

37. Q. What is the difference between a single-key tabulator, a decimal tabulator and a column selector?

A. A single key tabulator consists of one key which, when depressed, causes the carriage to jump from one tabulator stop to the next in rotation. A decimal tabulator works on the same principle but has five or six keys. The tabulator stops are set for units and the required key depressed for units, tens, hundreds, thousands, tens of thousands or hundreds of thousands. A column selector allows the carriage to "skip" over any number of set tab. stops. Depress the skip key and employ the tab. key just before reaching the desired position.

38. Q. In typing an engrossment of a deed you are asked to type the Testimonium Clause and Attestation Clause IN EXTENSO. What is meant by this instruction?

A. In an engrossment this means (a) the Testimonium Clause should be typed full out as follows: IN WITNESS whereof I have hereunto set my hand this —————— day of —————— One thousand nine hundred and ——————; and

(b) the Attestation Clause also full out:
SIGNED SEALED AND DELIVERED)
by the above-named ——————————)
in the presence of)

39. Q. What is meant by the term "stitching margin" when applied to a legal document?

A. A "stitching margin" means the small margin left on the right-hand side of every even-numbered page to allow the document to be sewn together without the words at the end of the lines being hidden.

40. Q. For what types of work are single, double and treble line spacing used?

A. Single line spacing is used for business letters, long specifications, plays, poetry, footnotes, insets, quotations and tabular statements.

Double line spacing is used for literary work, legal documents, short specifications, short business letters and drafts.

Treble line spacing is used for draft work which has to undergo extensive revision.

41. Q. Name two methods of making copies of letters sent out by a firm.

A. Letters may be copied by the carbon process or by a letter copier machine.

42. Q. When typing work not to be press copied would you use a record or a copying ribbon?

A. For work which has not to be press copied a record ribbon is used because a copying ribbon is liable to smear.

43. Q. If you have a large number of envelopes to type what method would you use in order to complete the work as quickly as possible?

A. The quickest way to type envelopes is to place all the envelopes on one side of the machine, flaps all the same way, and place face downwards on the other side of the machine after they have been typed. Also feed succeeding envelope in as completed one is taken from the machine, thus saving one operation. In typing foolscap envelopes it is customary to insert the envelopes with the flaps to the left.

44. Q. Why should copies of outgoing correspondence and letters and documents received be preserved?

A. Copies of outgoing letters are retained for reference as it is not possible to remember the details of every letter written, and letters and documents received are kept so that they can be referred to if a dispute arises.

45. Q. What do you understand by the term "combination characters"? Give three examples.

A. Combination characters mean two characters combined to make one character, e.g. $, ⅜, !

46. Q. What are the advantages of an Electric Typewriter?

A. The advantages of an Electric Typewriter are:
   Less energy is required.
   Greater speed can be obtained.
   Up to 20 carbon copies can be taken at one operation.
   All impressions appear the same irrespective of degree of touch.

47. Q. What are (a) Cardinal numbers?
              (b) Ordinal numbers?

A. (a) Cardinal numbers are 1, 2, 3 etc.
   (b) Ordinal numbers are 1st, 2nd, 3rd etc.

If these have been explained fully in this book the page number is given for reference. In cases where they have not been covered the answer is given.

1. Type the following, inserting full stops as required:

1st	inst	re	MSS	per pro
1st	inst.	re	MSS.	per pro.

2. Describe the course you would follow to feed a sheet of paper backwards into the machine. (p. 53)

3. Give four rules for dividing words at line-ends, and two examples of each rule. (p. 17)

4. Explain the meanings of:
   (a) the terms: sloping fractions (p. 51);
   hanging paragraph (p. 19);
   fit (p. 20)
   (b) the abbreviations: q.v., et. seq., cf. (pp. 22/23)

5. The typewriter is fitted with two devices for variable line-spacing. Explain the difference between the functions of these two devices. (p. 7)

6. What are "inferior" and "superior" characters? Type two examples of each. (p. 51)

7. What is meant by "reference marks"? Type three examples, and explain how they are produced when not provided on the keyboard. (p. 54)

8. When the typewriter ribbon and carbon sheets used are of different colours, how would you correct an error in the carbon copy after removal of the work from the machine? (p. 31)

9. Type the symbols or abbreviations you would use to represent the following:
   (a) compare (p. 22)   (b) section (p. 11)   (c) postscript (p. 23)
   (d) namely (p. 23)   (e) pages (p. 23)   (f) Members of Parliament
   M.P.s

10. Type in full the words represented by the following abbreviations:
    C.O.D.; B/L; c/f; (pp. 22/3) appro.;   Bros.
    approbation   Brothers

11. How do you obtain accurate registration when re-inserting typescript into the machine to finish a line already begun? (p. 54)

12. Type the following in their briefest forms:
    (a) pages (b) compare (c) which see (d) and the following (pp. 22/23)
    (e) G.P.O., B.E.A., B.B.C.—GPO, BEA, BBC
    (f) six hundred pounds and fifty pence—£600.50

13. Type the following in words and in roman numerals:

44	56	99	300	1,008	1958

forty-four   XLIV

fifty-six   LVI

ninety-nine   XCIX

three hundred   CCC

one thousand and eight   ..   MVIII

nineteen hundred and fifty-eight   MCMLVIII

14. When typing a quotation consisting of several paragraphs,
    (a) where would you place the quotation marks? (p. 16)
    (b) Type examples showing how you would indicate that a group of words
        had been omitted
        (i) from the middle of one of the sentences, and
        (ii) from the end of the quotation. (p. 54–5)

15. Explain the meanings of the following terms when applied to typescript:
    (a) Dropped head (p. 20)   (b) Fit (p. 21)   (c) Tail piece (p. 20)

16. How can you prolong the period in which carbon sheets will remain usable?
    (p. 31)

17. How should a copy of a single part (actor's copy) of a play be arranged? (p. 49)

18. What is the purpose of leader dots? What are the general accepted methods
    of typing them, and what rules should a typist observe when typing them?
    (pp. 45 and 54)

19. Distinguish between (a) a draft document; (b) a fair copy; and (c) an engross-
    ment. How should these documents be set out? (p. 21)

20. Name three points to be observed when typing a Balance Sheet which is
    to be typed on two separate sheets of paper. (p. 36)

21. Give four uses of the back-spacer. (p. 52)

22. Type the abbreviations that may be used to represent the following:
    manuscripts; that is; cash on delivery; pages; namely; for example.
    (pp. 22/23)

23. Express each of the following in words and in roman numerals:

50	936	40	19	1,000,000

fifty   L

nine hundred and thirty-six ..   CMXXXVI

forty   XL

nineteen   XIX

one million   ..   ..   .. $\overline{\text{M}}$

24. How many letters can be typed to the inch on machines which are supplied
    with (a) elite, and (b) pica type? How many lines in single-spacing can be
    typed to the inch? (p. 8)

25. Correct the following:

	Correct
re.	re
May & June were late.	May and June were late.
Mr. J. Ross, Esq.	J. Ross, Esq. *or* Mr. J. Ross
Miss Mary Barnes, L. R. A. M.	Miss Mary Barnes, L.R.A.M.

26. What precautions are necessary to keep your typewriter clean and in good working order? (p. 51)

27. Type the signs which may be used for the following;
caret; section; square bracket; double dagger. (pp. 11/12)
Explain when they are used.
The caret is a sign indicating the position of words or punctuation marks omitted or to be inserted.
Section is a sign indicating a division of a book, chapter or statute.
A square bracket is used to indicate a new paragraph; used in ms. work.
The double dagger is the third reference mark used to indicate footnotes.

28. Type the following statement using only signs and figures:
16.5 multiplied by 2 and divided by 4 equals 8.25
$$16.5 \times 2 \div 4 = 8.25$$

29. How is the *dash* represented in typewriting and in what way does it differ from the *hyphen*? (p. 52)

30. In addition to setting the margin regulator, what other precautions are necessary to maintain a uniform left-hand margin on successive sheets?
To maintain a uniform left-hand margin feed in each sheet of paper at the same place, i.e. against the paper guide, and return the carriage return lever to its fullest extent for each new line.

31. How is a typewritten copy of a letter distinguished from the original?
The word "copy" is typed in capitals at the top and the word "signed" typed in brackets before the signature.

32. Give four different uses of the full stop in typewriting. (p. 16)

33 Give four different occasions when it would be expeditious to use the tabulator. (p. 55)

34. Give two instances when it would be necessary to type within your left-hand margin.
For side headings in a specification and for characters' names in a play.

35. What is a "dead key"? What is its use? (p. 51)

36. When is it permissible to use the ampersand? (p. 12)

37. Give the meanings of the following abbreviations: et seq., i.e., viz., p.a., e.g. (p. 23)

INDEX